Making Visual Supports Work in the Home and Community

Making Visual Supports Work in the Home and Community

Strategies for Individuals with Autism and Asperger Syndrome

Jennifer L. Savner

Brenda Smith Myles

AAPC

Autism Asperger Publishing Co.
P. O. Box 23173
Shawnee Mission, Kansas 66283-0173

AAPC

© 2000 by Autism Asperger Publishing Co.
2005 Reprinted
P.O. Box 23173
Shawnee Mission, Kansas 66283-0173

Publisher's Cataloging-in-Publication
(Provided by Quality Books, Inc.)

Savner, Jennifer, L.
    Making visual supports work in the home and community : strategies for individuals with autism and Asperger syndrome / by Jennifer Savner and Brenda Myles. – 1st ed.
    p. cm.
    Includes bibliographical references.
    Library of Congress Catalog Card Number: 99-075479
    ISBN: 0-9672514-6-X

    1. Autistic children–Education.
    2. Communication–Study and teaching.
    3. Visual aids.   I. Myles, Brenda. II. Title.

LC4717.5.S38 1999   371.94
                QB199-1435

This book is designed in Minion, Khaki and Comic Sans

Managing Editor: Kirsten McBride
Editorial Assistant: Ginny Biddulph
Cover Design: Taku Hagiwara
Interior Design/Production: Tappan Design

Printed in the United States of America

As with the writing of any book of this kind,
the efforts of many people are involved.
Specifically, we would like thank the following individuals
for their assistance without which the writing of
this book would have been impossible:

Eric Biddulph

Gregory Biddulph

Thomas Biddulph

Natalie Dockhorn

John Durham

Elisa Gagnon

Ivy Gagnon

Taku Hagiwara

Tracy Hilgenfeld

Joe Mangino

Haley Myles

Kelly Tebbenkamp

In addition, we would like to thank the Mayer-Johnson Co. for allowing
us to use the Boardmaker™ and the Picture Communication Symbols.
The Picture Communication Symbols © 1981-2000, used with permission
from Mayer-Johnson, Inc., P.O. Box 1579, Solana Beach, CA 92075.
858-550-0084 (phone), 858-550-0449 (fax) and mayerj@mayer-johnson.com
Icons appear on the following pages:
i, ii, 3, 4, 5, 6, 8, 10, 12, 14, 15, 16, 17, 20, 22, 24, 27, 28 and 30.

JLS & BSM

Contents

Learning Through Seeing

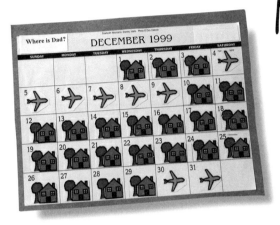

Most people learn in a variety of ways. They learn when they hear, when they see and when they experience something first hand. Often people prefer one method of learning over the others and try to use that method whenever possible. Although we may favor one method over another, most of us find that all three ways of learning are helpful.

Children with autism, Asperger Syndrome and other pervasive developmental disorders also learn in a variety of ways. But research has shown (a list of studies is included in the appendix) that for many children with autism and other similar disabilities, one way of learning – *learning through seeing* – is superior. Several studies have demonstrated that when children with autism spectrum disorders are given opportunities to learn with visual cues, they:

◆ learn more quickly

◆ reduce aggressive or self-injurious behavior

◆ decrease frustration and anxiety

◆ learn to adjust to changes at home and school

◆ complete tasks by themselves

◆ gain independence

Educators have developed and used visual supports to help their students achieve success in school and communities. Visual supports have helped students transition from one class to another, complete multi-step tasks, and follow rules and routines.

But what about the other 18 hours of the day, school breaks, weekends, and summers? Valuable information on visual supports is typically not readily

available to parents of children and youth with autism. Without sorting through research articles or lengthy books, parents do not have access to the information they need to help their child succeed at home. This book attempts to answer some of the questions parents have asked us about the use of visual supports. What are visual supports? Which ones do I use? How do I make them or get them? How do I use them?

This book was developed keeping in mind the limited time parents have to study to help their children. We realize getting through the day is in itself often an accomplishment. We hope that parents will be able to use this book successfully without involving a lot of time – time that they generally do not have. As a result, we have kept words to a minimum and maximized on visuals. We think that after you have seen the results of using visual supports with your child, you will be sold on this concept. We hope that, consequently, your child and your family will be happier and more successful.

JLS and BSM

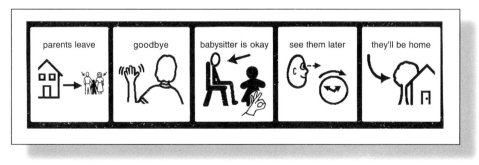

What Are Visual Supports?

Visual supports help children and youth with autism, Asperger Syndrome and other special needs understand their world better. Visual supports help children:

- follow rules

- understand what they are supposed to do

- know what is happening in their day

- understand how to complete work or play activities and tell someone they are finished

- move from one activity to another

- make choices about what they want to do

Diane Twachtman (1995), a well-known authority on autism spectrum disorders, defined visual supports as "a tool that enables the child to keep track of the day's events and activities and at the same time helps him or her to develop an understanding of time frame and an appreciation of environmental sequences" (p. 145).

Visual supports help children
and youth with autism,
Asperger Syndrome and other
special needs understand
their world better

Why Should My Child and I Use Visual Supports?

The best way for many children with autism spectrum disorders to learn is through pictures. In school, they use visual supports to see the day's activities, make choices, and understand rules. In daily life, adults also use visual supports. For example, we use calendars, daily planners, TV guides, movie listings, cookbooks, to-do lists, and maps to help us understand our world and complete our work on time.

Visual Supports Work

Many children with autism and Asperger Syndrome learn through seeing. In fact, many of us learn this way. Visual supports are useful to children regardless of their IQ and communication skills. They work not only for children who do not speak but also for those who do. Highly verbal children can benefit from visual supports. Some children can speak but cannot understand others' directions. For example, children with Asperger Syndrome may have good expressive language, but often do not process information that is given to them verbally. *Just because an individual with autism or a related special need can say the words does not mean that she understands them or knows what to do.* Even children who are severely cognitively challenged can learn more when they can see what it is they are supposed to do.

For many children, seeing a visual support is like having a light bulb go on in their head – they finally see the light and understand what you have been saying. According to Linda Hodgdon (1995), author of *Visual Strategies for Improving Communication,* "The use of visual communication tools is not determined by a student's ability to talk. These tools are valuable with both verbal and nonverbal students. Their use is determined in part by the students [sic] ability to take in information and make meaning from it" (p. 19).

The best way for many children
with autism spectrum disorder
to learn is through pictures

The Deciding Factors

The tricky thing about knowing when to use visual schedules is that your child usually will not say to you, "I do not understand. Please give me a visual." Instead, he will:

♦ not follow directions

♦ just stand there and look at you

♦ walk away

♦ tantrum

♦ continue doing whatever it was he was doing

♦ engage in other equally unattractive behaviors

For these reasons, your child, you, and your family may be constantly frustrated. And not only do you have to try to figure out how to help your child, you also have to endure the questions and helpful advice of well-meaning family and friends.

♦ "If you wouldn't spoil her, she would listen to you."

♦ "He knows he can get away with anything."

♦ "You know he knows what to do. He's done it a million times before."

♦ "She just wants her own way."

♦ "Just put your foot down."

If your child and you are experiencing frustration just trying to get through the moment and your child is resorting to some of the behaviors listed above, visual supports might make life easier for everybody involved.

You Can Do It!

It is possible to use visuals in the home to help your child. When you use visuals, you will find that your child becomes more successful and happy. It does, however, take a bit of time. Start small so you don't get discouraged. Create one visual support and see how it works.

Don't be afraid to ask for help. For example, your child's teacher may be able to show you a visual support that is used in your child's school. Or your local parent support group can plan a "make it and take it" session that includes a brief presentation and help in creating visual supports. Share ideas with one another. Copy the supports in this book. Chances are that the visual you need has already been created. If so, don't reinvent the wheel; copy it. But don't be afraid to change visuals to match your child and family needs. Remember to start small.

What Kind of Visual Supports Can I Use?

There are several types of visual supports that can be used in the home and community. They are similar in the way they look, but they serve different purposes. The most common visual supports include:

- visual schedules

- information sharers

- checklists/organizers

- visual behavior supports

Visual Schedules

Visual schedules set out the plan for the day, the morning, evening, or the week. They sequence activities for a certain period of time. The number of activities and amount of time shown on the schedule depend on your child's needs. Some children become anxious when they realize that they have 10 tasks to complete before bedtime. However, when they see what they need to do in a shorter time interval, for example, before dinner, they are fine. In this case, the child may have two visual schedules – one for before dinner and one for after dinner. Other children may need to see "the big picture." That is, they need to know everything they will be doing. You know your child and can decide which is better – a schedule that covers a shorter period or one that covers a longer period. If you are unsure, don't be afraid to ask your child's teacher what has worked well at school.

Visual schedules sequence
activities for a certain
period of time

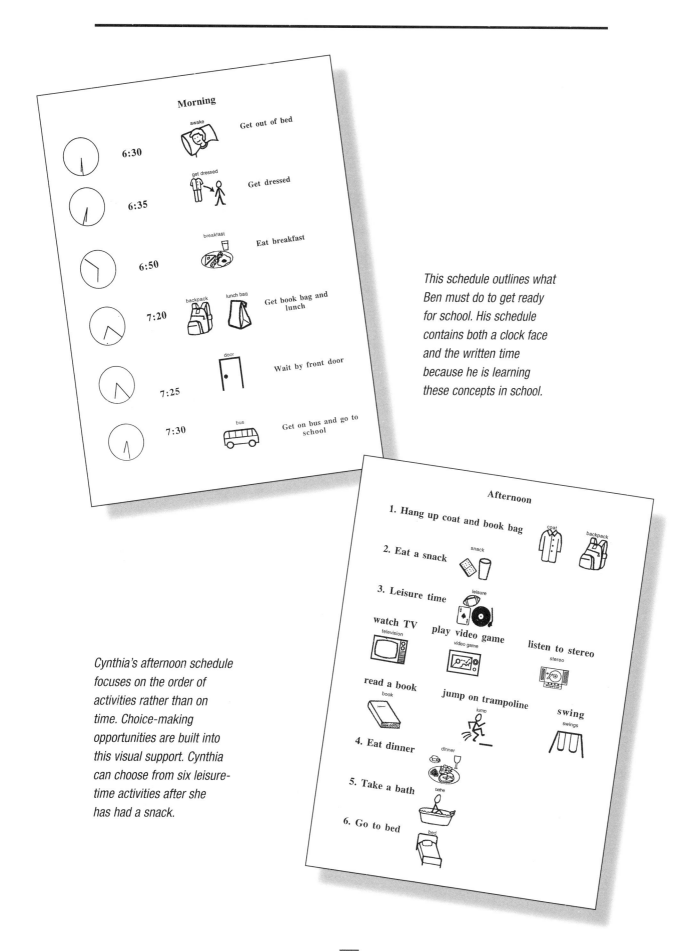

Morning

awake — Get out of bed — 6:30

get dressed — Get dressed — 6:35

breakfast — Eat breakfast — 6:50

backpack — lunch bag — Get book bag and lunch — 7:20

door — Wait by front door — 7:25

bus — Get on bus and go to school — 7:30

This schedule outlines what Ben must do to get ready for school. His schedule contains both a clock face and the written time because he is learning these concepts in school.

Afternoon

1. Hang up coat and book bag — coat — backpack

2. Eat a snack — snack

3. Leisure time — leisure

watch TV — television

play video game — video game

listen to stereo — stereo

read a book — book

jump on trampoline — jump

swing — swings

4. Eat dinner — dinner

5. Take a bath — bathe

6. Go to bed — bed

Cynthia's afternoon schedule focuses on the order of activities rather than on time. Choice-making opportunities are built into this visual support. Cynthia can choose from six leisure-time activities after she has had a snack.

This visual schedule, which can be easily posted on a refrigerator door, tells Sue the days she goes to school and the days she stays at home. Special appointments, such as Sue's upcoming trip to the doctor, also appear on the schedule.

This schedule is a regular photograph album, which contains activities that Ivy can do on the weekend. The photographs are easily removed, added, or reordered to match the family's plans.

Kaia had difficulty adjusting to a summer without visual supports. She relied heavily on them during the school year and without them did not have the structure she needed. Kaia and her mother took photographs of the things that she likes to do in the summer. After they were developed, Kaia and her mother labeled them and put them in a small notebook. Each morning, Kaia and her mother, father, or brother plan the day by ordering the photographs. Kaia's summer now has structure and she is much happier.

Just because an individual with autism or a related special need can say the words does not mean that she understands them or knows what to do

Many parents, including Karen's, report that haircuts are difficult for children with autism and Asperger Syndrome. Karen's hairdresser allowed the steps for a haircut to be photographed in her shop. Karen's mother keeps the pictures on a keyring in the glove compartment of her car. She and Karen review the pictures on the way to get Karen's hair cut. Since Karen began using these pictures, she has not tantrummed or cried during a haircut.

barber

When you use visuals, you will find that your child becomes more successful and happy

Inside this folder is an envelope that contains several pictures of free-time activities. Charles selects two that he can do each school day. His mother uses the same system at home. After school he selects the activities he will do prior to dinner time.

Information Sharers

One of the questions parents ask their child most frequently is, "What did you do today?" For many different reasons, children with autism spectrum disorders usually do not have a reply. They may not be able to (a) recall daily activities, (b) understand the question, or (c) organize their thoughts. Others, especially adolescents, may be experiencing the syndrome otherwise known as "I don't know"/"I didn't do anything."

Two types of information sharers will be discussed here:

♦ What I Did Today

♦ People Locators

A *What I Did Today* support easily goes from school to home to let parents know their child's activities. It serves as a conversation starter, helps reinforce what the child learned at school, and helps develop social skills like conversation turn-taking. In addition, this type of visual support helps keep the lines of communication open between you and your child's teacher. *What I Did Today* supports can also work in reverse, that is, they can be completed at home on evening activities and be sent to school.

Spencer uses this information sharer to tell his parents what he did at school. Spencer's teacher and Spencer circle all the activities he completed during the day. When Spencer gives the visual support to his father later in the day, they can talk about what Spencer did at school.

For children who are nonverbal or have difficulty relating the day's events, these information sharers made out of a baggie and school items serve as prompts for a parent to ask, "What did you do today?" The baggie contains items that represent the tasks or activities the child engages in.

For many different reasons, children with autism usually do not have a reply to the question, "What did you do today?"

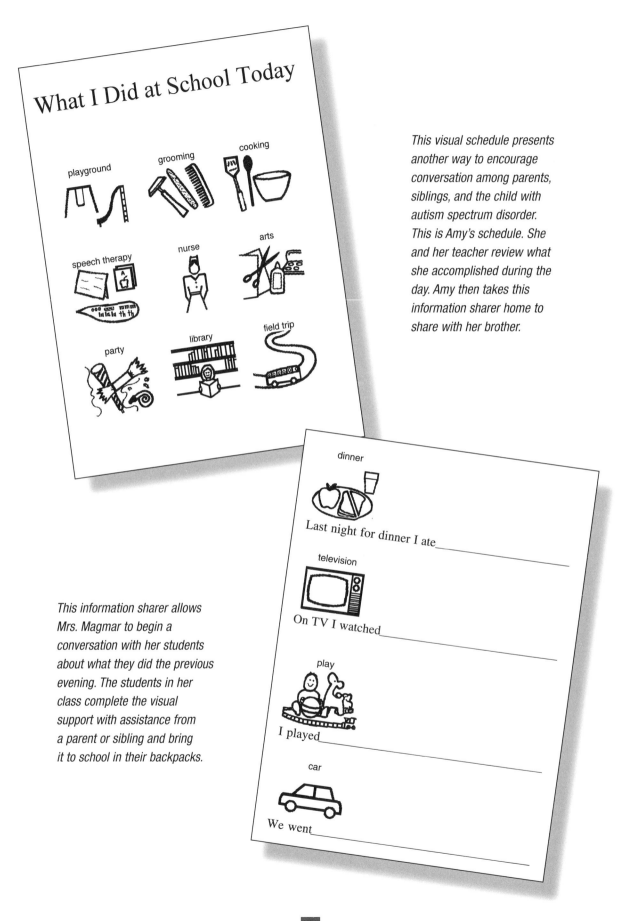

What I Did at School Today

playground

grooming

cooking

speech therapy

nurse

arts

party

library

field trip

This visual schedule presents another way to encourage conversation among parents, siblings, and the child with autism spectrum disorder. This is Amy's schedule. She and her teacher review what she accomplished during the day. Amy then takes this information sharer home to share with her brother.

This information sharer allows Mrs. Magmar to begin a conversation with her students about what they did the previous evening. The students in her class complete the visual support with assistance from a parent or sibling and bring it to school in their backpacks.

dinner

Last night for dinner I ate_____

television

On TV I watched_____

play

I played_____

car

We went_____

People Locators help children know where family members are. These are particularly important for children whose parents travel or who have a sibling away at school. A *People Locator* for a sibling away at college may contain a photograph of the college with a picture of the brother or sister. It may also include the date of the next visit home.

People Locators are also useful if a parent wishes to go out for an evening and a babysitter is employed. This type of *People Locator* may contain a photograph of the parent driving down the street waving good-bye, a picture of the babysitter with the child in the house, and a clock face showing the time when the parents will return.

This information sharer hangs on the wall in Sam's bedroom. It reminds him that his brother, John, is away at college. He also knows when he will see John again. Sam went with John when he first went away to college. In fact, he helped to take this picture.

My brother is at college.

The University of Kansas
Edwards Campus

He will visit me

My name is **Jennifer McBride.**

My phone # is **333-0890.**

I live at **32 Jones Drive, Olathe, KS.**

I am **6 years old.**

Jennifer, who is nonverbal, carries this card with her at all times. She has been instructed to show it to a policeman or store clerk if she gets lost. This information sharer helps Jennifer's mother feel more comfortable taking Jennifer on outings. One of Jennifer's behavior challenges includes running away from adults. Her mother believes that if Jennifer does run, this support will help keep her safe.

Lily was often anxious because she didn't know when her dad was out of town on business or in town. Lily now knows which days her dad will be at home and when he will be away. A side benefit of this schedule has been an improvement in Lily's counting skills. Lily and her mom count the days until dad comes home.

People Locators help children know where family members are

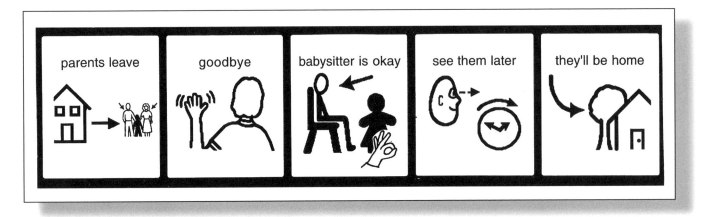

| parents leave | goodbye | babysitter is okay | see them later | they'll be home |

Mr. and Mrs. Smith use this information sharer when they go out for the evening. They review this visual support with their son, Ty, before they leave. Ty's babysitter, Kelly, refers to this information sharer throughout the evening as needed to assure Ty that his parents will be home later.

Checklists/Organizers

This type of visual support often breaks down the steps necessary to complete an activity. Some children with autism spectrum disorders are capable of completing parts of a task, but unable to organize themselves to complete the entire activity. Others have problems remembering exactly what they need to do.

In either case, a checklist/organizer is useful. It is a "how-to-do" manual detailing step-by-step directions that help the individual with autism complete an activity with minimal adult direction.

Checklists/organizers like this promote independence. Mark can wash his hands independently by following this support, which hangs in each of the family's two bathrooms.

Checklists/organizers break down the steps necessary to complete an activity

This checklist/organizer is one of William's cookbooks. William and his dad worked together so William could learn how to make a sandwich using this notebook of line drawings. Now whenever William wants a sandwich, he can get out his cookbook and help himself.

William also knows how to make popcorn using this photograph album cookbook his sister made.

Libby brings this checklist/organizer home from school the evening before a field trip. It helps her organize what she needs for the trip and prepares her for a change in the schedule.

Marj's dad sought permission from the local grocery store where he shops to photograph a typical shopping trip. He then placed the developed pictures in a small photo album, which he carries in the glove compartment of his car. Marj reviews her book on the way to the store. Her dad reports that Marj follows the steps in the book, and as a result pulling items off the shelf and running away from dad (two frequent occurrences prior to this checklist/organizer) are no longer major problems.

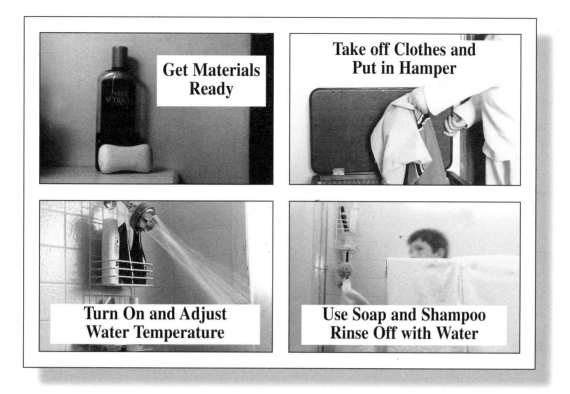

Get Materials Ready

Take off Clothes and Put in Hamper

Turn On and Adjust Water Temperature

Use Soap and Shampoo Rinse Off with Water

This checklist/organizer helps Thomas complete his bathing routine independently. Thomas' brother, a photography buff, took these pictures, had them developed, and posted them on a piece of cardboard. Thomas now completes his bathing routine independently following the checklist/organizer that is posted on his bathroom wall.

Lisa and her mother were exhausted by the time Lisa got ready for school each morning. Her mother was tired from constantly reminding Lisa what she had to do and Lisa was stressed from the commands her mother issued. Lisa wanted independence but often became side-tracked. Lisa uses this checklist every morning. As a result, Lisa and her mother are both happier and the day gets off to a good start.

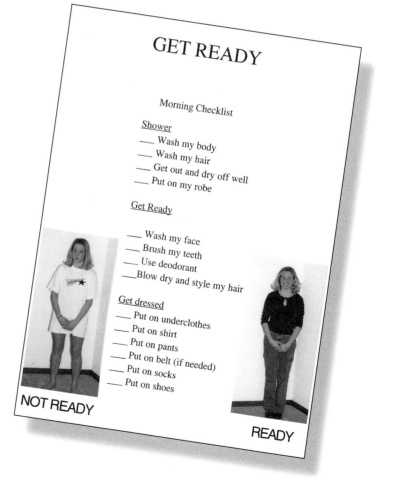

GET READY

Morning Checklist

Shower
— Wash my body
— Wash my hair
— Get out and dry off well
— Put on my robe

Get Ready

— Wash my face
— Brush my teeth
— Use deodorant
— Blow dry and style my hair

Get dressed
— Put on underclothes
— Put on shirt
— Put on pants
— Put on belt (if needed)
— Put on socks
— Put on shoes

NOT READY

READY

Visual Behavior Supports

Visual behavior supports provide the child with information on behavior expectations and possible consequences of following or not following the rules. In addition, it increases awareness and understanding of social situations.

A visual behavior support can specify rules for the dinner table or bedtime. It can also contain information for community outings. Information can be presented on 3x5 cards, business cards or in a notebook, depending on the child's needs.

Kristi has had a particularly difficult time using good manners at the table. Her mom and teacher worked together to create this visual behavior support that outlines table manners. Kristi and her mom read it before breakfast and supper, and Kristi reviews it with her teacher before lunch. It has helped make eating times to be more pleasant for everyone who eats with Kristi.

Manners for Eating

Use my fork or spoon to eat.

Take one bite at a time.

Chew my food with my mouth closed.

Chew my food and swallow it before taking another bite.

Wipe my face with my napkin.

Do not talk with food in my mouth.

Rules for Talking with Friends

1. When you want to say something to someone, say their name first to get their attention.
2. Always look at the person you are talking to.
3. Face the person you are talking to or turn your body towards them.
4. Always listen to what the other person is saying.

Reprinted with permission. From *Teach Me Language: A Language Manual for Children with Autism, Asperger's Syndrome and Related Developmental Disorders.* Langley, BC: SKF Books, Inc. (604) 534-6956.

All of the kids in Mrs. Williams' "lunch bunch" carry this card in their pockets or wallets. They have practiced these skills in their resource room and use this aid for generalization. On the playground, Jordan pulls this card out before approaching another child. Samantha reaches in her pocket and touches her rules card. This is enough of a reminder for Samantha to use the four rules.

Playing with my Sister

Gregory has difficulty sharing, particularly when playing with his sister, Haley. This visual behavior support outlines the rules for sharing. Gregory now knows when he should share and when he does not have to. Gregory and Haley's grandma reports that there are fewer fights between the children.

If we are playing with toys she can have one and I can have one and then we can trade. This is called sharing.

Eric thought the family television was exclusively his and tantrummed when anyone wanted to watch something of their choice. This visual behavior support gives Eric ideas of other activities that he can engage in when someone is watching a television show that is not of interest to him.

When I want to watch one TV show and everyone else is watching another, I can:

* Ask for help to record my show to watch later

* Get a book or magazine to read until the show is over

* Play by myself in the basement

* Go outside and ride my bike if it is still light outside

* Listen to music in my room

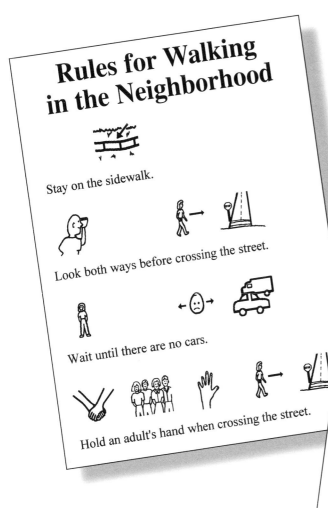

Rules for Walking in the Neighborhood

Stay on the sidewalk.

Look both ways before crossing the street.

Wait until there are no cars.

Hold an adult's hand when crossing the street.

Mary felt she was old enough to cross the street by herself even though she had difficulty remembering crossing safety. However, her parents didn't think she was quite ready yet and still needed adult supervision. Mary's dad and her teacher worked together to develop this visual behavior support, which they taught Mary to use whenever she goes outdoors. An 8 1/2 x 11 sheet containing the rules is posted on the doors in Mary's house. In addition, Mary has the rules on a business card that she always carries with her.

Although Jeff liked visiting Grandma, the trip to Grandma's house was usually less than enjoyable for everybody. Jeff had trouble with the concept of time. Even though his mother told him how long the trip was going to take, Jeff continually asked, "When are we going to be there?," and became increasingly agitated as the trip went on. In addition, he always wanted to sit in the front seat. Jeff's mom typed out this visual behavior support, which she and Jeff read every day for two weeks prior to the trip. Jeff also took a copy along during the trip. He read it several times on the way to St. Louis. His mother reported that it was their nicest trip yet.

Trip to Grandma's

1. On Saturday, October 16 we are going to visit Grandma in St. Louis.

2. It is 255 miles from our house to Grandma's house. It usually takes 4 to 5 hours to drive there.

3. We will leave our house at 10:00. For the first two hours I can ride in the front seat with Mom. I can choose what I want to listen to on the radio. I can play with my game boy or read a book.

4. At approximately 11:45 we will begin looking for a place to eat lunch. We may stop in Columbia at the McDonalds.

5. After lunch it will be my sister's turn to ride in front with Mom. She will get to choose what she wants to listen to on the radio. I will sit in the back seat. I can listen to tapes on the walkman or I can try to take a nap. Mom will give me a new word search book and a new yellow highlighter so I can choose to do that If I want to.

6. At 2:00 we will stop to get gas and buy a snack. Mom will give me $2.00 and I can choose what I want.

7. I will be happy when we get to Grandma's house. I will get out of the car and ring the doorbell. I may give her a big hug because I will be so glad to see her.

How Do I Make the Visual Support?

Making visual supports requires a time investment. As mentioned earlier, the rule is to start small. Make one visual support, see how it works and build upon it. For example, if the child's biggest difficulty is getting ready for bed, then create a visual that shows the child the steps to get to bed. After you have used this visual and seen how it helps your child and the rest of the family, create a second visual support that either addresses this area or another. That is, you may create a checklist on brushing teeth related to getting ready for bed. The brushing teeth checklist is likely to be more effective as it expands the child's getting ready for bed routine.

Making visual supports
requires a time investment.
Start small

Pictures

Many different types of pictures can be used when creating a visual support. When deciding on which picture type to use, keep these two guidelines in mind:

♦ the picture must match the child's ability level and be easily understood by both the child and others in his environment

♦ the picture must be easy for you to find or make.

Obtaining visuals does not need to be difficult. They are generally all around you. The trick is finding the one that matches the child's need. Here is a partial list of visuals that you can easily find at home or at work.

PHOTOGRAPHS – Instamatic, digital, disposable, or any generic camera can be used to take photographs. One type does not offer any real advantages over the other. An inexpensive generic or disposable camera takes pictures of a quality that is very adequate for a child to understand the visual support. Whichever camera type you use, be sure to take multiple pictures of each person, place, object, or activity step the first time around.

Keep visual support clear and concise,
including only the precise information
necessary to complete a task

That way, you can choose the picture that best represents what you need. Also, once you select the photograph(s) that will be used on the visual, get additional copies made. These can be used when (a) the original visual support is lost, (b) when you realize that the visual is needed in both the bedroom and the bathroom, or (c) the visual has been worn by repeated use. In addition, some pictures have multiple functions. For example, the toothbrushing picture can be used as a part of a visual support for getting ready for bed and getting ready for school.

MAGAZINE PICTURES – Finding magazine pictures for visual supports can be a family activity. Parents, children with exceptional needs, and their siblings can look for specific pictures together.

DRAWINGS – Even those of us without artistic talents can make drawings that can serve as visual supports. Stick figures or simple drawings are often easily understood by an individual with autism or Asperger Syndrome. Rather than simply taking advantage of these benefits, many adults are concerned that they cannot draw (rubbish!) and question whether they can even make a visual support; others get wrapped up in making detailed drawings. Remember: a simple drawing can communicate.

COMMERCIALLY MADE ICONS – Several companies make icons (line drawings that are either black/white or colored) that can be photocopied, which may be found in books or on computer programs. School district personnel are often good sources for commercially made icons and are usually happy to share this information with you. Boardmaker (Mayer-Johnson, 1981), Writing With Symbols 2000 (Mayer-Johnson, 2000), and Picture This ... (Silver Lining Multimedia, 1999) are examples of commercially made icons that are available in most school districts.

WRITTEN WORDS – Hand-printed or computer-generated words are a form of visuals. Often children simply need to see the steps for a given task or activity written out to understand what is expected of them.

dog

PAIRING – Most people find that it is effective to pair two different types of visuals. Typical pairs include some type of picture (i.e., photograph, commercially made icon, picture) and a written word or phrase. Again, any pairing decision should be made to best meet the child's needs.

As mentioned earlier, regardless of the type of pictures used, be sure to have more than one copy. The most important picture is always the one that disappears first! Placing pictures in labeled compartments in a storage bin will aid you in finding a needed picture quickly. Fishing tackle boxes or a compartmentalized hardware cabinet are ideal for storage.

Other Materials

Materials for visual supports are easily found in the home or school. With the exception of velcro and laminating material, most items resemble typical school supplies or may be found among the contents of the catch-all junk drawer common in most homes. A partial list of these materials includes:

- construction paper
- glue
- keyrings
- small photograph albums
- camera

- paper
- pencils
- crayons
- notecards
- tape

Velcro

Velcro may used in most visual supports. We recommend that velcro be purchased in bulk. Once you start using this material, the more you will need it. Helpful hint: before using velcro, create a "looped-fuzzy rule." Velcro has two sides: a looped side and a fuzzy side. Decide from the start that the looped side always goes on the back of the picture and the fuzzy side always goes on the item to which the picture is being attached or vice versa. It does not matter which option you choose, but it is important to implement your looped-fuzzy rule consistently.

Lamination

Using lamination or contact paper is often recommended to prolong the life of visual supports by enabling them to stand up to various types of destruction including chewing, drooling, adverse weather conditions or other kinds of destruction. Different weights of lamination or contact paper are available. Some allow the material to have a degree of "bend" or flexibility, while other weights are very sturdy. Decide on the weight depending on the intended use and the child's needs. Lamination is often available at office and teacher supply stores.

How Much Information to Put on the Visual Support

Keep visual support clear and concise, including only the precise information necessary to complete a task, both in pictorial and written information. Pictures need to focus on the most important or critical feature of the task. Pictures that include distractors do just that – **distract the child!** For example, a picture of brushing teeth should include (a) a toothbrush with toothpaste or (b) a close-up of the child's face with a toothbrush in or near the mouth.

Words also need to be direct. For example, words used to accompany toothbrushing may include: (a) put toothpaste on toothbrush, (b) brush teeth, (c) put water in the cup. Excess words create confusion. A few carefully thought-out words that describe the expectations are most effective. Words such as "appropriate" do not give a clear explanation of an expectation or task. A child does not necessarily understand what is meant by "brush your teeth in the appropriate place." She is more likely to understand "brush your teeth in the bathroom."

REMEMBER:
A simple drawing
can communicate

There is no one correct answer
to the question of which
behavior to target first

How Do My Child and I Use the Visual Support?

How to Choose Which Challenges to Address

Choosing which area or behavior to address is often the most difficult decision in using visual supports. There is no one correct answer to the question of which behavior to target first. For the parent who is not familiar with using visual supports, it may be wise to select a task the child has already mastered with adult prompts or guidance. For example, the child may be able to get dressed when the parent gives step-by-step directions or points to each item of clothing. If so, a visual support showing the steps of the dressing process requires only that the child learn how to use the visual support rather than having to learn a task and how to use the visual support at the same time. For the child who is already successfully using visual supports in a school setting, for example, parents may decide to select a relatively simple task as the first visual support.

A relatively easy task could be one that only includes a few steps, one that the child is highly motivated to complete, or one that does not need to be completed within a certain length of time. For example, the task organizer/ checklist "Making Microwave Popcorn" may be selected because it contains only a few steps and has a built-in motivator for the child – eating the popcorn when popped. Similarly, parents may wish to tackle a visual support related to going to bed before presenting a visual support on the morning routine, because the evening routine has fewer time constraints than the morning activity.

Other considerations include choosing a challenge that affects the whole family. For example, if having an evening meal and pleasant conversation

27

together is a high priority, a visual behavior support that outlines rules related to dinner etiquette might be important. If the child learns how to eat in a manner that is acceptable to the family and how to ask and answer questions, or otherwise participate in the family discussion, the evening meal could change from one filled with stress and anxiety to an enjoyable experience for all.

You may also want to select a strategy that will significantly impact the child's life. For example, having a friend or someone to talk with may improve the quality of life for an individual with autism or Asperger Syndrome. A visual behavior support that helps the child learn about "Rules for Talking with Friends," therefore, may be valuable. A safety issue, such as being able to provide others with name, telephone number, address or other personal information, may also be a primary target for a visual support.

Setting up the Support Together

As mentioned previously, parents, children with autism or Asperger Syndrome and their siblings can work together to make the visual support. For example, they can create or locate pictures as well as other needed materials and then together create the support. Many parents have reported that this is a fun activity. In addition to the support, parents have indicated that the process has helped their nonexceptional children.

Children with autism or
Asperger Syndrome and their siblings
can work together to make the visual support

Introducing the Support

Introducing the support is relatively easy, especially when the child has been involved in creating it. Parents can:

♦ talk with the child about the benefits, adjusting their language to the child's ability level

♦ model the steps of the process

♦ show the child a video clip of the process being completed using a visual support

Some parents have had their nonexceptional children create a "movie" showing the visual support in action.

Helping the Child Use the Support

Simply giving the child the visual support is not enough. Using a step-by-step format, an adult must teach the child how to use the visual support. The adult must model each step, prompt as needed, and always provide praise for attempts and successes.

Using the Support in Different Settings

It is important to determine what skills or activities can be completed in more than one environment. Generalization, an area of difficulty for children with autism and Asperger Syndrome, can be facilitated by a visual support. For example, the child can be taught to present safety information in the library, at school, or community to familiar adults or community helpers. "Rules for Talking with Friends" can be used on the playground or in the neighborhood. Similarly, a visual support of a bedtime routine can be used at home or on vacation.

How Will I Know if the Visual Support Works?

Teachers take data to know if an intervention works, plotting trends and directions. Parents also want to know if their efforts are paying off. But instead of recording data in an almost scientific manner, parents need something more practical.

Signs of Changes in Your Child's Behavior

1. Is your child tantrumming less often? Children often tantrum because they do not know how to do something. The visual support may have helped the child understand.

2. Are you finding that you have to repeat yourself less often? Does your child follow directions or respond to a request more often?

3. Have you noticed that your child has learned new and more positive behaviors?

Changes in Your Behavior As Well As Changes in Others Who Know Your Child and You

1. Do you feel less stressed when you ask your child to do something?

2. Does it feel easier to be at home and to go out into the community with your child?

3. Have those "well-meaning" family members and friends stopped making "useful" comments or giving "helpful" advice.

If you answer yes to some of these and similar questions, it is a sign that the visual support may be working. To be sure, you may also want to speak with your child's teacher to see if there is any carryover at school. Besides, it will help your child if the teacher knows what visual supports are successful at home and in the community.

When Do My Child and I Stop Using the Visual Support?

Too often we are quick to pull back on the use of visual supports when we see our children being successful. Remember, your child is being successful because you have provided him with and have taught him how to use these supports. Careful consideration must be given before removing support systems. Before totally withdrawing visual supports, it is a good idea to first modify them. Over time, the visual supports may become smaller, more easily portable, or be written at a higher level (i.e., using written words instead of a photograph). The visual support that was first presented in a three-ring binder using 8 1/2 x 11 paper and 4 inch pictures for your six-year-old may evolve into a business-card size visual support for your now teenager.

Think about yourself. Do you use a daily planner? Do you have a to-do list? What would happen to you if someone suddenly took your everyday tools away?

Careful consideration must be given before removing support systems

References

Freeman, S., & Dake, L. (1998). *Teach me language: A language manual for children with autism, Asperger's syndrome, and related developmental disorders.* Langley, BC: SKF Books.

Hodgdon, L. A. (1995). *Visual strategies for improving communication: Volume I: Practical support for school and home.* Troy, MI: Quirk Publishing.

Mayer-Johnson, R. (1981). *The picture communication symbols book.* Solana Beach, CA: Author.

Mayer-Johnson, R. (2000). *Writing with Symbols 2000.* Solana Beach, CA: Author.

Silver Lining Multimedia. (1999). *Picture this* . . . Poughkeepsie, NY: Author.

Twachtman, D. (1995). Methods to enhance communication in verbal children. In K. A. Quill (Ed.), *Teaching children with autism: Strategies to enhance communication and socialization* (pp. 133-162). Albany, NY: Delmar.

Appendix:
List of Articles Validating the Use of Visual Supports

Bainbridge, N., & Myles, B. S. (1999). The use of priming to introduce toilet training to a child with autism. *Focus on Autism and Other Developmental Disabilities, 14*(2), 106-109.

Hagiwara, T., & Myles, B. S. (1999). A multi-media social story intervention: Teaching skills to children with autism. *Focus on Autism and Other Developmental Disabilities, 14*(2), 82-95.

Krantz, P. J., MacDuff, M. T., & McClannahan, L. E. (1993). Programming participation in family activities for children with autism: Parents' use of photographic activity schedules. *Journal of Applied Behavior Analysis, 26,* 89-97.

Kuttler, S., Myles, B. S., & Carlson, J. K. (1998). The use of social stories to reduce precursors of tantrum behavior in a student with autism. *Focus on Autism and Other Developmental Disabilities, 13*(3), 176-182.

MacDuff, G. S., Krantz, P. J., & McClannahan, L. E. (1993). Teaching children with autism to use photographic activity schedules: Maintenance and generalization of complex response chains. *Journal of Applied Behavior Analysis, 26,* 89-97.

Norris, C., & Dattilo, J. (1999). Evaluating effects of a social story intervention on a young girl with autism. *Focus on Autism and Other Developmental Disabilities, 14*(3), 180-186.

Pierce, K. C., & Schreibman, L. (1994). Teaching daily living skills to children with autism in unsupervised settings through pictorial self-management. *Journal of Applied Behavior Analysis, 27,* 471-481.

Swaggart, B. L., Gagnon, E., Bock, S. J., Earles, T. L., Quinn, C., Myles, B. S., & Simpson, R. L. (1995). Using social stories to teach social and behavioral skills to children with autism. *Focus on Autistic Behavior, 10*(1), 1-16.

Vaughn, B., & Horner, H. (1995). Effects of concrete versus verbal choice systems on problem behavior. *Augmentative and Alternative Communication, 11,* 89-92.